In God's Presence

A Book of Poetry

Lanre Adetula

World rights reserved. This book or any portion thereof may not be copied or reproduced in any form or manner whatever, except as provided by law, without the written permission of the publisher, except by a reviewer who may quote brief passages in a review.

The author assumes full responsibility for the accuracy of all facts and quotations as cited in this book. The opinions expressed in this book are the author's personal views and interpretations, and do not necessarily reflect those of the publisher.

This book is provided with the understanding that the publisher is not engaged in giving spiritual, legal, medical, or other professional advice. If authoritative advice is needed, the reader should seek the counsel of a competent professional.

Copyright © 2018 Lanre Adetula

Copyright © 2018 TEACH Services, Inc.

ISBN-13: 978-1-4796-0958-1 (Paperback)

ISBN-13: 978-1-4796-0959-8 (ePub)
Library of Congress Control Number: 2018942607

Image Credits: Cover-Leonid Tit; Ring The Bells-Balakate; Bruised Hands-Gino Santa Maria; On Eagles Wings-Halibut; My Protector-aslysun; Persecuted-Thawornnurak; Folusho-digitalskillet1; War!- Zeferli/BigStockPhoto.com

Acknowledgements

All glory be to my Heavenly Father and His Son, the King of Glory, Yeshua, the Source of my inspiration! I thank the Father for:

Andrew, my loving and dependable husband.

Folusho, my joyful and cherished daughter.

Iyabo, my sister, confidante, and friend, who is a source of numerous blessings to me and our family (nuclear and extended);

Femi, my mother, a living manifestation and testimony of "faith not fear" no matter the circumstances—she is a constant example and the one I run to after prayer for my most difficult situations.

Chief Adetula, my father, who always told me how intelligent and beautiful I was.

Ade, my brother, for his positivity.

All of my **nieces**, **nephews**, and **in-laws**.

Adrianna for her friendship.

Shmuel Wolkenfeld, whose ministry opened my eyes to who and whose I am in Yeshua.

Pastor Jones for taking care of me when I needed it the most.

My **brothers and sisters in the Lord** and my experience at the Central SDA Church, Salt Lake City, UT; Your Bible Speaks SDA Church, Portland, OR; Beacon Light SDA Church, Kansas City, MO; Agape SDA Church and Northside SDA Church, both in St. Louis, MO.

Every individual the Father has caused to cross my life path—we may not have understood His purpose, but it was definitely for a reason.

To Heavenly Father, be all the glory, honor, and power. Amen.

In God's Presence

In God's Presence
I want to continually be
So it only makes sense
That I pray unceasingly

I speak to Him as I wake up
I listen for Him as I lay down
On my knees, hands raised up
From my lips not a sound

My heart cries out to Him
My mind praises Him
My soul depends on Him
My God, Father, Friend, and King

With each step I take
Throughout the day
With each plan I make
He has full say

In God's Presence
I'm committed to be
Only in Him do I find peace
By His Grace I am truly free

Ring The Bells

Ring the bells
The saints are coming in
Ring the bells
Lord Jesus leading in
Throw the gates open wide
Hold your victory palms high
We are marching

Ring the bells
Lord Jesus is our King
Ring the bells
Praises to Him we sing
Praise Him heart, mind, and soul
Forever praise Him all creatures here below

Ring the bells
Lord Jesus died for me
Ring the bells
With Him forever I will be
I'll live with Him through eternity
And serve His almighty Sovereignty
Humbly, totally, and completely

Ring the bells
In Him I am victorious
Ring the bells
This experience is glorious
Being in His Presence
Beyond human ability to express
Intoxicating and converting is His very Essence

Ring the bells
The vision has come to an end
Ring the bells
Till this world truly ends
As He comes majestic in the clouds
And the trumpet loudly sounds
As angels take each Christ-child
homeward bound

When His Glory Is Revealed

The earth will quake
Mountains will shake
The dead in Christ will awake
Those faithful to the end will He take
When His Glory is revealed

There will be nowhere to hide
But kings and nations will try
Those who pierced Jesus' side
Will in awe be terrified
When His Glory is revealed

The oceans will roar
The angels and saved will soar
Transformation of saints will occur
The world as we know it will be no more
When His Glory is revealed

The trump of God will sound
There will be angels all around
The Archangel will cry out loud
The saved will be lifted off the ground
As His Glory is revealed

The coming of the King is near
Those who have ears let them hear
All those who are already aware
Must with all those around them share
His Glory soon to be revealed

Holy Sabbath Rest

Lord God I thank you
For Your holy Sabbath rest
During this sacred period
I worship You best

Spiritually, mentally, emotionally
You draw me close
In Your Presence physically
I experience sure repose

From sunset to sunset
In awe my focus is You
Since Your Commands I respect
Your Sabbath I will not forget

My Father, My God
My Creator and King
My dates with You
Such joy they bring

I can only imagine
What the future will bring
At this very hour
I witness and experience Your Power
My heart full of joy
In praise can only sing

In Jesus Name

In Jesus Name
I am free
In Jesus Name
I will be everything He has called me to be

In Jesus Name
I have faith
In Jesus Name
On the Lord I will wait

In Jesus Name
I have peace
In Jesus Name
Beyond my understanding it will not cease

In Jesus Name
I have joy
In Jesus Name
It will endure as I abide in Him now and forever

Thank you Lord for freedom
Thank you Lord for all I've overcome in You
Amen

Yeshua

Creator of the earth, wind, and skies
So soon Your Glory will arise
In majesty with heavenly hosts
All eyes will see from coast to coast
His second coming glorious, zooming through Orion
Third coming powerful, feet parting Mount Zion
Sun of Righteousness with celestial beings
All creation prepare to meet your heavenly King
Fire in eyes
Sword in mouth
Crowns on woolly hair
Bronze arms and legs
Gold colored sash
On white horse seated
Intensely dramatic
Righteous liberation
Sin forever destroyed
Earth made new
His Holiness eternal habitation

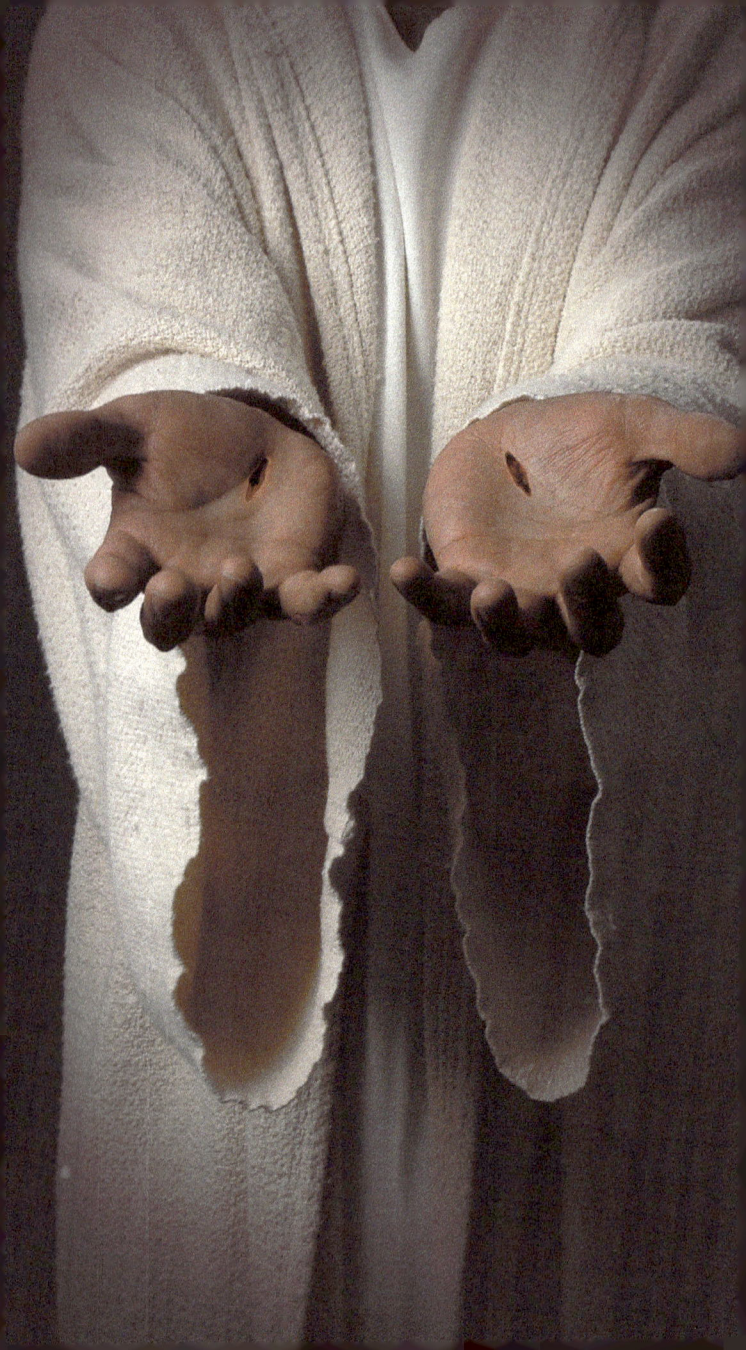

Bruised Hands

I will be resurrected if I sleep

I will be lifted up in the air

Changed in the twinkling of an eye

So of death I have no fear

Why so confident you ask

Why so sure of the future to be

Because of His death on the cross for me

His bruised hands proof for all to see

All My Eggs In One Basket

I put all my eggs in one basket
I have no fears
No thoughts of regret

All my eggs in one basket
Without a doubt
Great things I expect

All my eggs in one basket
Not one out
Did I forget

All my eggs in one basket
Not very smart
You wanna bet?

All my eggs in one basket
Multiplied, pressed down
Running over harvest

When all your eggs are in God's basket
You're guaranteed
Nothing but the best!

His Coming

A tremendous thunderous roar

Bolts of lightning traverse the sky

Mountains split east to west

North to south

Spews of fire, winds of smoke

Trumpets blast, turbulence in the air

Orion parts, chariots approach

Clouds everywhere with colors

Bursting forth ambers, bronze, rainbows

Here at last the King

Creator and Lover of our soul arrives

Time of Trouble

To the mountains
I will flee
From the cities
Safe I will be

In His Care I'll surely rest
No more fear
During the test

Coming soon Lord Yeshua
Though You protect and You provide
And Your Spirit ever guides
I yearn Your Presence by my side

Oh the humanity of me!
Your Holy Spirit dwells in me
Yet my longing and desire constantly
Your hand to hold, Your face to see

Sabbath

The Sabbath day I like the best

Because I am blessed to rest

To rest

And pray

And play

With God

And family

And friends

For one whole Holy Day

Father's Throne

Swirls o' violets, indigo, green. orange, red, blue, and yellow

Wrapped around the gigantic throne

Footstool the earth

Backrest reaching to the heavens

Fiery tongues of fire

Blue, red, yellow, and orange

Dancing, moving, shooting out

Going Home

I look forward to rising up in the air

In the wings of my angel

Feel the air move against my skin

As I rise toward the stars

Stop and visit different worlds and beings

As I float to my destination

See Yeshua, Adam, and all my ancestors

As we finally journey home

Stones Cry Out

Jesus made it clear
My Glory will be declared
By stones if you won't
Well, what could they possibly say?

Mount Everest declares
My God is the Alpha and Omega
The First, Last, and Best
In Him you'll find solace and rest

Mount Kilimanjaro proclaims
He cares for the sparrow
You don't have to wallow in sorrow
Have no fear, not even of arrows

The Grand Canyon declares
The Lord God is One
Breathtaking and awesome
A Beauty you cannot fathom

The Rocky Mountains declare
The Smoky Mountains roar
The Appalachian Mountains concur
In harmony they announce the Lord's Grandeur

The Black Hills of Dakota
Declare God is here
Isn't that all we need
His ever-loving Presence and care

Beauty Of My Jesus

The Beauty of my Jesus
I am here to share
The Beauty of my Creator
The Son of God so fair

Here's an inkling of the reflection
Of my God and King
The Beauty apparent in His creation
Yet fall short as breathtaking as they seem

The flaming orange flamingo
And the enchanting blue sea
The majestic redwoods
The royal blue iris I see

The brilliant multicolored sunsets
And striped yellow black jacket bees
The handsome black-tie penguins
And everything green

Need I say more?
What for?
I could but I won't
For it is written:

No eyes have seen
Nor ears heard
Neither can the heart imagine
The Beauty of my King

On Eagle's Wings

To fly on eagle's wings
Away from the worries that the world brings
I thank the Lord for His marvelous way out
And all I have to do is wait

I shall run and not grow weary
I will in fact only get stronger
For a while I thought I couldn't go much longer
Till You reminded me that all I have to do is wait

I shall walk and not faint
I'm trying to be patient but I'm no saint
I'm trying to keep still because You are God
From fear, reverence, and obedience that's why I wait

Wait, wait, wait
For what do I wait?
They that wait on the Lord shall renew their strength
Strength I need so for that I do wait
Endurance I need so for that I do wait
To see You in all Your Glory
Is certainly worth the wait

My Protector

I call upon the Lord in prayer
My heart calls out from a deep need
To remain continually under Your Wings
To be safe and protected do I plead

This world is scary and full of danger
But with Your Holy Spirit living in me
I know peace is my portion and never fear
Because Your Presence is ever near

You're my ever-present Help when I'm in trouble
Left for me I'd live in a bubble
Not one of plastic made with human hands
But one of social isolation and fear of man

Lord Jesus I thank You for Your Care
For if not for Your Blood
I wouldn't be here
I'd be lost and confused and scared to death
When I need to be still and know You are near

My Present Help

Lord You're my very present Help in time
of trouble
You're the Alpha and Omega of my needs
You're my Warmth and Provider when I'm alone
On cold nights You are my Shelter from the storm

You're my very present Help in time of trouble
You're my Protector and my Shield from all I fear
You keep me safe from danger and my foes
With You I need have no doubts nor any fear

You're my very present Help in time of trouble
You're my King, my Creator, and my Friend
You know me in and out, You love me all the same
You're my Father, my Mother, You're everything
that I need

You're my very present Help in time of trouble
With You I know I can't go wrong
You lead and guide and keep me in Your path
of righteousness
And by Your grace someday
I will dwell in Your Holiness

Till then in Your Presence
I will remain

What Is God To Me?

What is God to me?
A Shelter from the storm
The Provider of all that I need
My Guide when I think I can see

What is God to me?
He is my Guard and my Shield
My only Protection from Danger
An impenetrable, strong Tower

What is God to me?
My Help, my Strength
Who keeps me up when I should be down
And keeps me safe with chaos all around

Who is God to me?
My Creator, my Father
The Lover of my soul
The One who keeps me whole

Who is God to me?
My Brother, my Husband, my Savior
My Everything and All
But at His feet I'm unworthy to fall

Dedication

Lord I come before You in praise
I kneel and bow before You
To You alone my hands I raise
In adoration and reverence for all that You do

Lord God full of Majesty and Grace
Yet Meek and Kind, and Strong and Mild
In eternity we'll see face to face
Till then to You only do I prostrate

Lord my God to You only do I pray
To Your will and Your laws
I humbly submit to obey
For You're my God and King, the Holy One above all else

My heart, mind, and soul I commit to You
My body acceptable is my goal
A living sacrifice approved by You
A ministering witness in all that I do

Praise

All I can do is praise You
When I look up at the sky so blue
Lord I thank You for being so faithful
As I look at the sky of stars so full

Lord You are worthy
Please accept my praise
My God in wisdom You are mighty
Help me to do what Your Word says

You are my song
Because of You I have joy
With You I can't go wrong
That's why in praise I lift up my voice

Thank You Father
Halleluyah!
I lift YOU higher
I magnify You, Sir

My soul sings out to You
Glory, Halleluyah
My heart rings praises too
Hail Almighty Father

Persecuted

Oh Lord in this cell I rot
My flesh, my organs, my bones
My soul cries out in praise to You
My heart gives thanks for all that You do

The pain, oh Lord, is more than I can bear
A wonder Lord that I am still here
I ponder anew Your Death on the cross
Ah! I'm walking in Your Footsteps my Savior
and Boss

My spiritual ancestors were burned at the stake
Dismembered, disemboweled, tortured,
and hanged
Denounced and rebuked as though they made
a mistake
To accept Jesus the Word as the only Savior and Lord

I look to You Lord from whence comes my help
Which in this case would be speedy death
Escape from the hook and whip and failing health
On meeting my Savior, I am dead-set

Thank You Lord for the sun I no longer see
Thank You for my guardian angel standing here
with me
Thank You Lord for Your soon coming to take
me home with Thee
Thank You Lord from this world, by You I'll be
set free

Persecution

Let's remember believers in China and Indonesia
And various countries in Asia
Christians enduring such pain
It's enough to drive them insane

Throughout the world
Christians are under the sword
For what they firmly believe
Because the Holy Spirit they have received

Christians who are not ashamed
When before the world arraigned
Facing the present world which bears a frown
But looking to the future when they'll receive
a crown

O Lord how long must they stand
Having their blood spilled on blood-soaked land
In Africa, Arabia and Europe, too
Perpetrators unaware by the adversary
They're being used

The end, My children, is soon to come
When all suffering will be brought to an end
And a new world dawns
When I, Your Savior, enter in and reign
As King in the New Jerusalem

A Tool In My Father's Hand

A useful tool in my Father's hands
I am determined to be
An instrument for healing
That especially my patients see

When the body is broken
And there seems to be no hope
The Son appears with healing in His Wings
Perfectly fitting the pieces together again

He lifts the despairing spirit
Restoring peace in people like you never expect to see it
For He is the Great Restorer
A Miracle Maker to say the least

Only He can heal the tormented soul
Or bring back the living from the dead
Only He can see beyond the surface
And fill the bottomless needs of the human spirit

My God is the Healer of us all
He is the Great Physician
Who brings about healing
Physically, mentally, emotionally, and spiritually

Folusho

A miracle of God you truly are
How you survived I have no idea
Stuck in the womb with competition
One pound heavier
With bumps and lumps
And no way out
Limited food to eat
Limited room to move and breathe
Almost from the start to the very end

A child of God you truly are
He preserved and presented you
Hand crafted, beautiful, and complete
Made to order, right on time
To fulfill your designed purpose
As you bring Him glory, pleasure, and praise

I Seek Help

Lord for the events about to unfold
I seek help!
For the salvation of my family and myself
I seek help!
To be closer to You Lord
I seek help!
To be in Christ in God
I seek help!
To be Your favored child
I seek help!
To be in Your Will continually
I seek help!
For the unrevealed and things not clear to me
Help me, Lord Almighty, please help
As You usher me into Your Presence
For all eternity
I thank You, Lord, for all Your Help
Halleluyah!

Help Me Love You

Lord help me to serve YOU faithfully
Remind me to consult YOU consistently
Nudge me to follow Your Lead
Speak to my hearing and help me to listen
Give me understanding that I might obey

Help me to be obedient
Living according to YOUR Word
Give me a desire for YOU
And a love for You that surpasses all other
Instill a loyal love that meets Your Desire

Help me to keep my focus on YOU
Lord be the Center of my world
Everywhere I look I want to see YOU
Inhabit my heart, my mind, and soul
That I may continually experience You

Thank YOU, Lord for helping me
For dwelling in one as lowly as I
A Spirit King, Creator God, Grand and Mighty
Undeserving though I be
You surely, truly do love me

Focus On The Priority

Jesus the One and Only Healer
Forgive me for thinking I can heal
Lord You are my soul Provider
So why do I depend so much on my trade

Lord I work so hard
I suspect that's not Your plan
Work is good, but You are better
Like with Mary you prefer our time together

When I make You the Priority
And my patients secondary
Only then will the great Physician
Bring about complete recovery

When I spend more time with You
Only then am I available
Because I am in touch with You
To be of use and pliable

Lord keep focus on You
Not on what You've asked me to do
So that each and every patient
Will experience Your Loveliness
And depart feeling closer
To Your Presence and Holiness

Work Prayer

Dear Father in Heaven
My only Safe Haven
As I leave for work right now
In my car I humbly bow
I ask that You go before little me
And visit each patient I plan to see
Bring about healing, oh Lord, I pray
And give me wisdom for every word I say
Words of compassion, patience, and grace
That reflect the brilliance and beauty
Of Your beautiful Face
Bless me in all that I think, say, or do
And good Lord may all the glory go to You
Bless all that I put my hands upon
As I humbly kneel before Your Throne
Show me my mistakes, point out things I'd overlook
Help me document exactly by the book
Turn errors into blessings
Make my very presence uplifting
Teach me to relate to patients, colleagues, staff
and nursing
After dealing with mere me
May all without a doubt know
That they have been in contact with You
The Creator of land and sea
May You receive all the glory my God
All honor and praise "Halleluyah"
To You all majesty and power
Amen!

War!

What can pills do for a mind that is ill?
Medicine, surgery, the latest medical gadget
What can these do for an Army Sergeant
In whose eyes are reflected such terror
From fighting and experiencing war and its horror

In the face of war
Things seen unthinkable
Experiences felt unimaginable
Scenes going through the mind unstoppable
And like Noah's ark, unsinkable

Difficult situations of sickness and pain
Missing limbs with leaky veins
Children, women, casualties of war
Carried away in a flood of blood

After all these years I find
That any and all healing of the mind
Must originate from the Creator of mankind
Only the Maker of the mind can
fully comprehend
And mend, and to all pain bring an end

Lord be with these officers
In all that they do
Keep and protect them
As they trust in You

Source Of Healing

Lord God in heaven
A doctor I claim to be
Under this facade
Only You can see

To help and to heal
I took an oath
Of course You were there
For every exam I wrote

My Lord in humility
I have a favor to ask
That You will go before me
For each and every task

Bring healing to patients
Before I ever act
Without You there can be no healing
I know that for a fact

Thank You Lord for hearing my prayer
Thank You for responding to my plea
My patients are getting better
And that's all I need to see

The "P" Prayer

God of Avraham, Yit'chak, and Ya`akov
The Great I AM
The Creator of heaven and earth and sea
Father Lord God I pray:
For Your **Presence** in my life
Fill me with Your Holy Spirit
For Your **Peace** in my mind and heart
Let it flood my soul like a river
For your **Protection** Lord I pray
Over my mind, body, spirit, finances, heart,
and soul
For Your **Provision** Father I pray
May I always give You praise when I'm full
For Your **Power** Lord I pray
Move me and use me to the glory of Your Name
For Your **Purpose** for my life I pray
That all Your **Plans** for my life be fulfilled
And not one talent be wasted
For Your **Presents** for my life I pray
That the gifts You bestow upon me
Will draw multitudes to You, Father
Prosper me that abundant Fruit of the Spirit
be **Produced**
And Your children be blessed through me
Prepare me for Your coming
May Your **Praise** be continually on my lips
In Yeshua's Name I pray
Amen

Inspire Me

Lord give me songs to sing

So that praises to You I'll bring

Glory, Glory, Glory my King

Now and forevermore will ring

Baba

Tall, dark, and elderly
Handsome as could be
Sun weathered skin, not a wrinkle in sight
All thirty-two teeth his, even though not one white

Tall, muscular, and strong
Though one hundred and six
A farmer to the end
Ate fresh fruit and veggies which he fixed
Fresh meal and roots straight from the land

A healer, a hunter, and kingmaker by birth
Born of Hebrew parents who had a godly influence
A devout Muslim till the truth he heard
Accepted Messiah at one hundred and four

A tobacco chewer for years
Smoked a pipe from the age of six
With only blackened teeth to show for it
Grew old on whole foods from the land he picked

He never lost his eyesight
And always stood upright
Had fun going up and down the stairs
No matter how many flights

An old man with a quick temper
Who forgave and forgot even quicker
Not from dementia as one would expect
But from Christ influence in a God-fearing heart

He stopped smoking tobacco
And the occasional gin drinking too
When his life to Christ he gave
To forever more be saved

Tall, venerable, and dignified
Respected by youth and elders alike
Trusted in God all his life
Probably why he lived so long

Thank You Lord for my grandpa
I didn't learn all I could from him
But I loved him and still do
Through all the elders I speak to

He's dead and asleep for now
When I see him again it'll be WOW
Translated and transformed
Tall, dark, strong, and handsome
And so much younger than now

Hope

God's alive

No matter what You're going through

His loving Arms around you

When He comes back

He'll take you

To live then and forever more

Don't let go of hope

Hold on to the lifesaving rope

That's Yeshua without whom we can't cope

In Him we live and stay afloat

Despite The Odds

A mover, shaker, doer, survivor
A woman of stature
A tremendous miraculous success
In spite of the odds
All thanks to God

The loss of a mother
Devastating like no other
At a tender young age
The oldest of four girls
So soon the farewells

Father, a farmer and hunter
Did his best to provide shelter
But alas! with no money
For school fees to pay
Determination got her through the day

Got through high school
For she was no fool
Labeled a debtor by peers and superiors
Yet determined in school to stay
As she kept debt collectors at bay

Got married to get ahead
The hunger for a college education fed
Struggled with three babies
And graduated as well
With honors. how swell!

A job well done
But yet more miles to run
Three sisters still in need
Emotionally, physically, and financially
With dreams to someday, somebody be

Hurray! It's done
And everybody won
The sisters, the children, the woman too
Hard work with accomplishments to show
Drudgery and hardships not always the foe

A prayer warrior, the subject matter
A woman of faith, my precious mother
Intelligent, powerful, successful by God's Grace
Showered with God's tremendous Blessings
With immense gratitude her heart daily sings

What came first?
The chicken or the egg?
Did determination beat the odds or did the odds breed determination?
With God in control we need never know

Spouse

A man with strapping good looks
A perfect husband and a very good cook
Always ready to go the extra mile
A servant leader with a ready smile

Strong yet kind, a God-fearing man
Who strives to stay in touch with the Master's Plan
Of his home the high priest who
continually intercedes
Under the gentle and perfect guidance of
the Holy Spirit

Dependent on the touch and steer of
the Master's Hand
He's captain of his ship, a man of much worth,
an ideal husband
Morning and evening he's in the Word
Knowing the only protection of his home is God's
two-edged Sword

He is lord and master of his home
Whose utmost role and decided goal
Is to keep his family in safety
Under God the Father's protective dome

Ade

My younger brother
He's all about order
He's kind and loving
And sharing and caring

He has come so far
And has a lot to offer
He does not recognize his progress
But by God's Grace he will not regress

He's a husband and father
Progressed from just son and brother
He's responsible and a provider
Faithful lover and hard worker

A good dancer
Haven't seen any finer
Making money
He takes very seriously

When Jesus in the clouds returns
And brother stands before the throne
I pray he won't try to run
But will from the Father hear "Well Done"

Polygamy

A polygamist, father, and farmer

Who really didn't care for some of his family's welfare

Loved some more than others

It was glaringly clear

Home was not welcoming to all living there

Sad and true, the story of life

What does a man do with more than one wife

Always one favored, resulting in strife

Amongst children and wives

Into the prime of their lives

Fighting against the very happiness

For which they all strive

Abba

My father and friend
Mild to hot tempered, yet gentle
With always a listening ear to lend

Easy to converse with
A sense of humor
Just as easy to laugh with

He in me instilled
A healthy sense of self
By little things done, and loving words said

Always ready with a helping hand
Teaching his daughters
Things generally reserved for men

Aging gracefully
And handsomely too
Getting better every day, in every way

I love my daddy
I always will
Through him Christ's Love, so tangible and real

Loss Of Sister

The loss so hard to bear
A sister alone with no one there
Supposedly in the doctor's care
But went to sleep with no nurses there

I am so sad my heart could break
This pain in my soul so hard to shake
I really wish I would awake
And of all this a bad dream make

I miss my sister so I cry
As each day passes I wonder why
Even though all must die
I never did get to say goodbye

Dear Lord I stand upon Your Word
I trust my sister and I will be of one accord
When death loses to Your two-edged Sword
And You rule eternally as King and Lord

Moi

My name is `Lanre
I am the daughter of the Most High God
The Great I AM
The Creator of the heavens and the earth
The Elohim of Avraham, Yitc'hak, and Ya`akov
Whose only begotten Son is Yeshua, my Messiah
His Name is YHWH
Blessed be His Holy Name
Whose Kingdom is from eternity to eternity

TEACH Services, Inc.
P U B L I S H I N G

We invite you to view the complete
selection of titles we publish at:
www.TEACHServices.com

We encourage you to write us
with your thoughts about this,
or any other book we publish at:
info@TEACHServices.com

TEACH Services' titles may be purchased in
bulk quantities for educational, fund-raising,
business, or promotional use.
bulksales@TEACHServices.com

Finally, if you are interested in seeing
your own book in print, please contact us at:
publishing@TEACHServices.com

We are happy to review your manuscript at no charge.

www.ingramcontent.com/pod-product-compliance
Lightning Source LLC
Chambersburg PA
CBHW042137160426
43200CB00019B/2960